LOCKE IN 90 MINUTES

Paul Strathern

LOCKE
(1632–1704)
in 90 minutes

Constable · London

First published in Great Britain 1996
by Constable and Company Limited
3 The Lanchesters, 162 Fulham Palace Road
London W6 9ER
Copyright © Paul Strathern 1996
The right of Paul Strathern to be identified as author
of this work has been asserted by him
in accordance with the Copyright,
Designs and Patents Act 1988
ISBN 0 09 476000 4
Set in Linotype Sabon by
Rowland Phototypesetting Ltd,
Bury St Edmunds, Suffolk
Printed in Great Britain by
St Edmundsbury Press Ltd,
Bury St Edmunds, Suffolk

A CIP catalogue record of this book
is available from the British Library

Contents

Introduction

Philosophy moves backwards. It began with an infinite universe of complex, beautiful and often conflicting ideas. Gradually, with the aid of religious bigotry, reason and the will to understand, philosophy began to shrink this world to more comprehensible proportions. Everything became simpler, more obvious. Philosophy was regressing towards the point where it described the world as we actually see it. With John Locke philosophy enters its flat earth period.

Great ideas are often obvious. None more so than those of John Locke. Much of his thought we would now regard as common sense. His philosophy was to lay the foundations of Empiricism, with its belief that our knowledge of the world is based on experience. It also introduced the idea of liberal democracy, which has become the shibboleth of Western civilization. People who can't even spell philosophy are now liable to accept these philosophical tenets, which were incomprehensible just over three centuries ago.

This all makes Locke's philosophy rather uninteresting. But there's no reason why philosophy shouldn't be dull. On the contrary, there are very good reasons why it *should* be. It was when philosophical works became interesting, and people actually began reading them, that the trouble started. People who read things are liable to believe in them, and then look what happens. The earlier part of the twentieth century remains as a hideous reminder of what happens when large groups of people start taking philosophy seriously. Fortunately, the discipline has now progressed well beyond the infantile stage where people who read it are expected to believe in it. But this was not always the case – and many of the wisest philosophers have realized the pitfalls of readers actually understanding what they are saying. Spinoza did his best to solve this problem by rendering his works unreadable. Socrates, on the other hand, decided that the best way was not to write anything down at all. (The former course was adopted by philosophers such as Kant and Hegel, the latter by Polique, Ehrensvard and Huntingdon-Jones.) Locke's solution was to write philosophy that was so obvious it soon appeared dull. But it wasn't always so. Locke's thought and ideas were revolutionary in their time, and altered the course of thinking.

Locke was the only major philosopher to become a government minister. And it shows. He was a man of many parts, but he remained for the most part consistent and practical. His philosophy is one that actually works – for both the individual and society at large.

Life and work

Locke attempted to live a life that was almost as dull as his philosophy. Fortunately for us, though not for him, he lived in exciting times – and couldn't avoid getting involved. John Locke was born on 29 August 1632 in a small rather grubby thatched cottage by the church in the Somerset village of Wrington. His father was an unambitious country lawyer and his mother a tanner's daughter, who was reputed to have been a great beauty. Soon after John Locke's birth his parents moved to a family property near the small market town of Pensford, just south of Bristol. Here Locke grew up in a Tudor farmhouse called Belluton. This actual building has long since disappeared, but the present house which occupies the site is said to have been built on its foundations. It stands on a hill above the rather ordinary little town of Pensford, but here on a summer's day you have a breathtaking view out over the Mendip Hills in the direction of Midsomer Norton and Downside Abbey.

This rural idyll was shattered by the outbreak of the Civil War in 1642, when John Locke was ten. The war was the culmination of a long-standing dispute between King Charles I and Parliament. Charles believed in the Divine Right of Kings, according to which the monarch received his authority direct from God, and was thus not answerable to institutions run by mere mortals, such as Parliament. The members of Parliament, who were responsible for voting the king his cash, thought otherwise. In fact, the Civil War was basically a stand-up fight between the emerging mercantile class in the red corner, with the king and his landed aristocracy in the blue corner. It tore the country apart, and was to bring about the first successful revolution in modern European history.

The Locke family supported the Parliamentarians. The local member of Parliament, Alexander Popham, became colonel of the regional Parliamentary militia, and appointed Locke's father as his captain. Locke's father left home to join the campaign. After coming across a few unsuspecting Royalist columns, which they quickly put to flight, Colonel Popham's militia joined up with the Parliamentary army at Devizes. But this time the Royalists were prepared, and in the ensuing rout Locke's father and Popham were lucky to escape with their lives. After this they 'decided to withdraw from the military life', and returned home.

By now the country was in a turmoil, and as a result Locke's family found themselves without means of support. Colonel Popham did his best for his old captain, but only managed to secure him a post as the county clerk for sewers (this may well reflect how both these ex-warriors were held in local esteem).

In 1646 Charles I was captured, and three

years later he was beheaded. The Commonwealth was set up, with Oliver Cromwell soon emerging as its head. Meanwhile Colonel Popham MP was able to do a further favour for his friend Captain Locke. As a member of Parliament he was allowed to nominate pupils for entry to Westminster School in London, the finest in the land at the time. This favour, granted to the son of an obscure impecunious West Country lawyer, was to change John Locke's life. Without such an education it is doubtful whether Locke would have had the opportunity to realize his exceptional talents.

Curiously, although Westminster was controlled by a Parliamentary committee it retained a Royalist headmaster. This was a failed actor called Dr Busby, who was renowned for his dramatic and sadistic floggings. According to the poet Dryden, who was a contemporary of Locke's at Westminster, 'our Master Busby used to whip a boy so long, till he made him a confirmed blockhead'. However, the essayist Steele who was also a pupil was of the opinion that Busby had 'a genius for education'. And, astonishingly, this is the view which has prevailed. Two centuries later the prime minister Gladstone commended Dr Busby as 'the founder of the public school system'.

John Locke was a frail youngster, and the prospect of an encounter with Dr Busby doubtless stimulated his dormant intellectual faculties to the full. As one of the brightest scholars at Westminster, Locke would certainly have got to know the precocious Dryden, who was already publishing poetry before he left school. Dryden appears to have learned something from his Royalist headmaster's survival technique – in a school which stood in the very shadow of Parliament, during a time when the king was executed just across Parliament Square in Whitehall. At the age of twenty-six Dryden was to write a heroic tribute to Oliver Cromwell. Two years later when the monarchy was restored, Dryden composed an equally mellifluous celebration of Charles II, and was later rewarded with the post of Poet Laureate. Whilst Poet Laureate he composed a paean to the Anglican church; but when the Catholic James II ascended the throne he changed his mind, became a Roman Catholic, and wrote an epic celebration of Catholicism. Unfortunately this time he was caught out, because a few years later the Protestant King William took over the throne, and Dryden was stripped of his Poet Laureateship. All this is far too interesting to be anything to do with John Locke, but it serves to illustrate the frequent (and often dangerous) switches of political fortunes which were to take place during his lifetime. Unlike the great poet, Locke was to regard his principles as something more than a weather vane. Even so, they were to undergo several transformations. The first of these took place during his schooldays at Westminster. Locke had been brought up in a staunchly Parliamentarian home, but at school he found himself making friends with a number of Royalists amongst the pupils. These encounters, as well as his dislike of Parliamentarian excesses (such as the execution of the king), led him to a more sympathetic view of the Royalists. Learning from experience and toleration, the two things for which Locke was to become renowned, were already apparent.

Yet in other ways Locke was a slow starter. He may have been bright at school, but he showed no signs of intellectual giantism. Indeed, he didn't leave Westminster until he was twenty (the age at which his contemporary Leibnitz was already being offered a professorship). In 1652 Locke enrolled as an undergraduate at Christ Church college, Oxford. Education at Oxford University remained in the medieval era. Undergraduates were required to address their tutors, and each other when in hall, in Latin. The curriculum was limited to the study of the classics, logic and metaphysics. Despite the new philosophy of Descartes and recent widespread advances in science and mathematics, Aristotle and Scholasticism reigned supreme. Undergraduates had the worst of both worlds, for even the time-honoured benefits of a medieval education had been abolished. A short while previously the bordellos and low-life taverns of Oxford had been closed down by the aptly titled vice-chancellor of the university.

The curriculum of non-stop Classics and Scholasticism was so boring that even Locke was driven to seek elsewhere for intellectual stimulation. He began taking an interest in chemical experiments and medicine. Experimental science had recently been introduced to Oxford by John Wilkins, but it remained a fringe interest. It was viewed with much the same intellectual disdain as present-day universities tend to regard ESP or economics, and its introduction to Oxford had long been opposed. (The fact that Wilkins was Cromwell's brother-in-law may well have helped in initially overcoming this opposition.)

Locke was introduced to medicine by his former schoolfriend, Richard Lower. Medical knowledge was still largely based on Aristotle and the Ancient Greek authorities, such as Galen and Hippocrates; but some felt the need to extend this knowledge by scientific investigation and experiment. These had already led to great advances in the study of anatomy – such as Harvey's discovery of the circulation of the blood. (As a result of this, Locke's friend Lower undertook a daring experiment – daring for his patient, as much as himself – and became the first man to perform a successful blood transfusion.) Even so, for practical purposes medicine remained largely at the sawbones and leeches stage.

Locke read avidly of the latest developments, but refrained from taking up medical carpentry as a hobby.

By this stage the Commonwealth was being run by the Puritan element, and the country was beginning to suffer from the post-revolutionary religious fanaticism which has now become the norm, even after atheist revolutions. The English have always been very good at being boring, and several times in their history have emerged for considerable periods as undisputed world masters in the field. This was one of them. Under the Puritans all conspicuous signs of enjoyment were rigorously banned. Even Christmas was banned – despite what it celebrated. Citizens were expected to work all day, and spend the rest of their time conforming. Life was given over to Party indoctrination, the thought police, informers (on the likes of wicked Christmas-pudding eaters), and long sessions spent studying the principles of Markism,

Lukism and Johnism. Until in the end even the English had had enough, and decided to invite Charles II to take over. They preferred to be ruled by a drunkard who lived with a prostitute, rather than do without Christmas pudding.

Meanwhile Locke's father had fallen seriously ill. Locke learned that he was being treated by the celebrated Irish doctor Edmund Meara, and wrote to his father expressing his confidence that he was in safe hands and would soon recover. This is curious as Dr Meara was already notorious for having denounced Harvey's discovery of the circulation of the blood as a hoax, and had written a virulent pamphlet attacking Locke's pioneering medical friend Lower. As a result of Dr Meara's attentions Locke's father soon got worse, and within a few months he was dead. Though Locke did travel down to Somerset before the end (and even called in a new doctor), his behaviour here remains inexplicable.

Could he have harboured some (perhaps unconscious) resentment against his father? Locke's father had been strict at home, but could well have lost authority when he was temporarily ruined by the Civil War. In later life Locke always referred to his father respectfully, but as it was his habit to keep his deeper feelings to himself we can only speculate.

As a result of his father's death Locke inherited a parcel of land and some cottages. The rent from these provided him with an income on which he could have lived modestly for the rest of his life. But Locke had no wish to become a gentleman. By now he had graduated and become a don at Christ Church. The Restoration had brought with it a new libertarianism, and Locke took advantage of this – in his own prudent fashion. He began casting his eyes around at the ladies (who wished to be known as such in those days, and usually behaved like them – except

at the royal court and in Restoration come-
dies). To judge from the portraits we have of
Locke, he was an oddly handsome man, in a
rather austere distinguished manner. Though
this may have been offset by his constant poor
health. He appears to have suffered from
asthma since childhood. Some have attributed
this to psychosomatic causes, and indeed
there may have been tensions in his childhood
home. A good-looking mother of lower social
standing married to an unambitious sometimes impecunious man ten years her senior,
who spent long periods away fighting in the
Civil War or inspecting the county's sewers,
hardly seems a recipe for domestic bliss. But
asthma didn't stop John Locke's roving eye.
Unfortunately, Locke had been brought up in
a Parliamentary household which espoused
Puritan ways. Though he had by now trans-
ferred his sympathies to the Royalists, he
never fully abandoned his former allegiance.
At heart, something of the Puritan ethic

remained – both in his behaviour, and also in his choice of ladies. He would write them long intricately coy letters, and they would reply in equally amorous fashion. I quote from a typical example:

Worthy Sir,

You are not able to imagine with what content and satisfaction I read over your civil and most obliging letter . . .

I am sorry to hear that you rode out of your way, and repent with grief that I should be the cause of it, for I assure you that it was my prayers that you might have a happy journey . . .

And so on, ending: 'I remain your cordial friend . . .'

Locke replied a week later: 'That my returns are not so quick as yours is owing to an impossibility of finding that ecstasy your excellent letter first put me into, for which a week's time is but little to recover myself.'

Unsurprisingly, not much came of these often prolonged dalliances, which were sometimes daringly conducted with more than one lady at a time.

But Locke may well have been a little disingenuous about the reasons for his week-long delay in replying to his cordial friend. Despite his poor health he set himself a heavy schedule, and read long into the night.

Ostensibly Locke may have been a lecturer in Ancient Greek, but he still devoted most of his time to scientific studies. However, although he remained theoretically in favour of practical experiment, in practice his studies remained purely theoretical.

Science appears to have fulfilled a deep need in Locke. Like his country, he remained deeply divided between the 'unreflective adhesion to tradition' of the Royalists, and the 'enthusiasm' (i.e. unexamined emotional fervour) of the Puritans. Science was Locke's way out of this dilemma. Here was a subject which relied purely upon experience (rather than tradition), and arrived at its truths through experiment (rather than fervent conviction).

Locke's reading of rational science eventually led him to the rational philosophy of Descartes. Here at last, at the late age of thirty-four, he discovered his subject. It was Descartes who gave him 'a relish of philosophical studies'. Descartes' thinking was to have a decisive influence on Locke. Indeed, to this day some French commentators consider him as one of Descartes' followers. But this is ridiculous – as is shown by Voltaire, who rejected Descartes but was heavily influenced by Locke.

Locke certainly appreciated Descartes' importance in overthrowing Aristotle and putting an end to centuries of stifling Scholasticism. He also admired Descartes' method. In order to arrive at an indisputable bedrock of truth, Descartes doubted the evidence of his senses and even the workings of his mind. He arrived at his famous conclusion: '*Cogito ergo sum*' (I think, therefore I am.) On this foundation he then reconstructed a surer world by means of reason and deduction. Locke accepted that Descartes' method did away with many accepted notions and pre-conceptions, but his instincts were scientific. He mistrusted Descartes' reasoning and deduction as a method of arriving at the truth about the world. In Locke's view this could only be discovered by induction: *scientific* method.

Locke was encouraged in this view by the French thinker Gassendi, one of Descartes' most penetrating critics. Gassendi was a mathematician of some brilliance, but it was in his life that he managed to square the circle. Gassendi succeeded in combining the roles of priest, philosopher and scientist. As a philos-opher he espoused Epicureanism (which didn't believe in a life after death) and as a scientist he was the first to observe the planetary transit of Mercury around the Sun (when the Pope still decreed that the sun and the planets circled the earth). In his capacity as a Catholic priest, one can only wonder how he managed to reduce this circular thinking to the square of Catholic orthodoxy.

Gassendi insisted that all knowledge was based on sensory perception. For Locke, this was the equivalent of Descartes' *cogito*: it was to be the foundation on which he built his philosophy.

Locke never acknowledged his debt to Gassendi. This is very much in character. Throughout his life Locke remained an inordinately secretive man. In his notebooks he used a coded form of shorthand, as well as various inscrutable ciphers. When he received letters he was in the habit of deleting or excising altogether names and places. Even when writing to his women friends he sometimes used invisible ink in his more suggestive passages. Though it must be stressed that this is very much a relative term where Locke is concerned. ('If the opinion which tells us that everyone has his tutelar angel is true, I am confident that you are mine, seeing that I find that under the protection of your company I am not only the happier but the better, too; and that those evils which assault me in other places dare not approach me while I am near you,' is alas as risqué as he gets, invisible ink or no.)

Locke may have attempted to hide his debt to Gassendi, but this secretiveness also led him to deny altogether another cardinal influence on his thought. Whilst he was still an undergraduate Locke had read Hobbes' authoritarian political masterpiece *The Leviathan*. In this Hobbes put forward the pessimistic view that without government 'the life of man [is] solitary, poor, nasty, brutish and short'. Human beings had found this state of nature unbearable, and had congregated together in governed societies to overcome it. Any form of government was better than none, and thus we should obey whoever is in charge.

Locke had found himself agreeing with this. 'The magistrate of every nation, what way so ever created, *must necessarily have an absolute and arbitrary power over all the indifferent actions of his people.*' This was an understandable view during the troubled years following the Civil War, in the midst of 'this great bedlam of England'. Yet it was a far cry from the toleration which was to be the cornerstone of his later philosophy. Over the years Locke's ideas gradually evolved away from this early view, but he always denied that it was Hobbes who had first influenced him and inspired him to think about political philosophy.

By the time Locke had become a don at Christ Church, his thoughts on political philosophy had begun to deepen. In 1663 he wrote, but didn't publish, a paper entitled the *Law of Nature*. This marks a decisive stage in Locke's thought, boldly linking philosophy and politics – in a way which had not been done before, and has seldom been usefully improved upon since. Locke suggested that the vital element in all political problems is the nature of human beings, and that to understand this nature we must first discover how human beings arrive at their knowledge of the world they inhabit. Subsequent attempts to ignore this profound link between philosophy and politics have usually resulted either in inhuman philosophy or inhuman politics.

As we shall see, these problems lead directly to Locke's later philosophy, and also to his more optimistic view of man's basic nature.

After four years of dalliance with Oxford ladies and teaching Ancient Greek, Locke decided to strike out for fresh pastures. In

1665 he secured an appointment as secretary on a diplomatic mission to Brandenburg. Judging from his letters home he didn't much like the foreign grub, which was 'more a mess than a meal'; and on one occasion he was even served 'a piece of powdered beef covered with preserved quinces', which was far too Germanic for his tastes. Despite offers of further diplomatic work he returned to his rooms at Oxford. Here he went on reading the latest works by Descartes and pursuing his amateur interest in medicine – taking care to avoid going out too much in case he caught the Plague, which was raging through the country at the time.

It was at Oxford that Locke met a rather ugly little aristocrat who was to play a decisive role in his life. Lord Ashley was less than five foot tall, but a man of forceful character. He was also a daring and astute politician. He had originally supported the Royalists, but switched sides in the middle of the Civil War when he suspected that Charles I was planning to sell out to the Catholics. During the Commonwealth Ashley was appointed by Cromwell to the Council of State, but later fell out with his boss. In 1660 Ashley was one of the party sent by Parliament to tell Charles II to come home – all is forgiven. At the time Locke met him, Ashley was one of the most powerful political figures in the country. Ashley seems to have taken to Locke from the word go. Within no time he had appointed the philosopher as his personal physician. Despite the fact that Locke had no qualifications for this job, he successfully delivered Ashley's wife of a child. When Ashley began suffering from a suppurating abscess of the liver, you'd think that Locke might have called in a doctor. But not a bit of it. After consulting a couple of medical treatises he decided to operate. A surgeon barber was summoned and ordered to slice open his lordship, whereupon Locke inserted a silver tube to drain the abscess. Lord Ashley continued to wear this tube for the rest of his days, and was convinced that Locke had saved his life. Amazingly, he almost certainly had.

Besides serving the Ashley family as a quack, Locke also acted as tutor to the children, and even carried out negotiations for the marriage of Lord Ashley's son. Aristocratic English marriages, like those between central European peasants, were invariably arranged with much hard bargaining between the two families involved. For peasants and bluebloods alike, breeding qualities, land and cash were usually the main considerations – the aesthetic merits and finer feelings of the participants being as little considered as they were evident. After completing the customary horse-trading, Locke secured a suitable contract and the marriage went ahead.

Locke was now living in London, and was able to hold regular meetings with his intellectual peers. Here they would discuss the latest philosophical and scientific developments (such as how a man can survive with a silver tube inserted into his abdomen). Locke also wrote another political paper, his *Essay Concerning Toleration*. In this paper he asserted that no one knows enough to dictate to another the form of his religion; that to compel an individual against his will only achieves lip-service conformity; and that we are all responsible to God, which not only makes us moral beings but also presupposes our freedom. The fact that these original views now appear to us as pious commonplaces reflects on Locke's wisdom rather than our judgement.

Things were very different in seventeenth-century England. Locke prudently decided against publication of his *Essay Concerning Toleration*, which would almost certainly have guaranteed him a lifetime behind bars in any country in Europe (with the possible exception of liberal Holland). But this was the essay which contained the seminal ideas which he was later to develop in his master-piece of political philosophy, *Two Treatises of Government*.

In 1672 Ashley was made Lord Shaftesbury and appointed Lord Chancellor, which was then the highest political post in the land. Lord Shaftesbury (as he is usually known in the history books) had always looked upon Locke as more than just his personal physician-cum-matchmaker. He frequently sought Locke's advice on political and intellectual matters. (In those far-off days these two elements were not mutually exclusive.) Shaftesbury and Locke held much in common, especially their attitude towards the benefits of foreign trade and their views on toleration. (Though in Shaftesbury's case the latter had a considerable lacuna. He didn't believe in tolerance towards Catholics, and is recalled by one historian as being 'one of the most passionate anti-Catholics in English history'.)

Shaftesbury now had the good judgement to appoint Locke to various posts in the administration, and for a couple of years Locke became secretary to the newly formed Council of Trade and Plantations. As a result Locke was able to put his political theories into practice, when he helped to draft the constitution for the colony of Carolina.

Locke's ideas on liberal democracy were to have a more lasting effect on political philosophy than any others in the history of this notorious so-called science. It may be the anti-heroes such as Machiavelli, Louis XIV and Marx who grab the limelight, but it is Locke whose ideas are embodied in the United States constitution, the British constitution (as well as all those modelled on it), and even for a brief period the French constitution.

Locke continued to discuss his ideas with his intellectual cronies, and after one particularly disputatious evening with 'five or six friends meeting at my chambers' he decided to try and set down his philosophical ideas in a coherent form. These were eventually to constitute the basis of his masterwork *An Essay Concerning Human Understanding*. When I was recently looking through the first edition of this work in the British Library I came across a note in the margin. This was written in a shaky hand in fading sepia ink, apparently by Locke's friend Tyrrell, and it referred to that original meeting in Locke's chambers: 'This was in the winter of 1673 as I remember myself being one of those.' That historic evening could be said to have marked the start of Empiricism – the first philosophy since the origin of the subject over 2,000 years previously to take the radical step of basing itself on experience.

From now on, for the next twenty years, the problem of human knowledge, how we come by it, and what precisely it is, was to remain Locke's major concern. But by 1675 Locke's asthma had deteriorated to the extent that he could no longer continue living in London. The air, heavy with coal dust, smoke and fogs plagued his lungs. Long fits of coughing and wheezing would often reduce him to a state of exhaustion. Locke was forced to give up most of his administrative work and retire to Oxford, where he was still nominally a don at Christ Church. Around the same time Lord Shaftesbury fell from favour with the king and was dismissed. Locke then left for France, allegedly on account of his health, but almost certainly to carry out some politicking for Shaftesbury as well. Locke was to remain in France for four years. Here he came into contact with the Gassendists (followers of the scientist-priest Gassendi, who had died twenty years previously). They favoured the experimental approach adopted by Kepler and Galileo, believing in a science based on atomic particles. Like their master, they rejected both Scholasticism and Descartes, in favour of an empirical and hedonistic approach (though the latter may appear sadly theoretical to modern sensibilities). The idea that we learn through experience, and the principle that in social philosophy pleasure must be seen as good, continued to play a major role in Locke's thinking.

During this period Locke appears to have acted on occasions as a tutor to the sons of English aristocrats, and to have travelled extensively throughout France. Locke's health continued to bother him, and drawing on his extensive medical researches he eventually diagnosed himself as suffering from phthisis – which causes wasting of the body, especially the lungs. The health resort of Montpellier was renowned for curing phthisis, and at one stage Locke travelled here to take the cure. But this was of little avail, not least because of Locke's mistaken self-diagnosis. On his travels, he continued to complain about the food. At one stage he arrived at an inn where 'the whole bill of fare' was 'nothing but cabbage and a frog that was caught in it and some haws [hawthorn fruit] of last season'. He didn't take to the French much either (men all had the pox, Jesuits sleeping with the nuns etc.).

While Locke was travelling on the newly opened Canal du Midi between Toulouse and Agen he had an accident, 'a great pole having fallen on my head in the boat'. But he had recovered by the time he arrived back in Paris, where he saw Louis XIV and his queen at the opera. He also had another chance to put his (still unqualified) medical skills into practice. The British ambassador's wife had become delirious with agony as a result of a tooth-ache. Her (qualified) French physician had already pulled out two perfectly good teeth to no avail. Locke examined the patient and diagnosed trigeminal neuralgia – apparently the first diagnosis of its kind in medical history. He prescribed a violent purge, which astonishingly did the trick. (As a cure for toothache, was this too a first, one wonders.)

When Locke returned to England in 1679 the country was in the grip of a political crisis. Charles II was intent on making his Catholic brother James the heir to the throne, and Shaftesbury was leading the Parliamentary opposition to this move. Shaftesbury had already been locked up in the Tower for his troubles, but was now back in favour with the king. He had been appointed Lord President of the Privy Council, and was attempting to affect a reconciliation between Charles and Parliament. In the midst of all this Locke sent Shaftesbury a paper entitled *Observations on the Growth and Culture of Vines and Olives*, with the aim of 'demonstrating that it is possible for something good to come out of France'. Unfortunately Shaftesbury didn't have much time to study this fascinating document as he was arrested on a charge of treason, through the machinations of his enemies. (Amongst these was Locke's old school friend Dryden, who immortalized Shaftesbury in his *Absalom and Achitophel*, which was not only the finest satirical poem to appear in the seventeenth century, but also one of the most wrongheaded.)

Locke was now almost fifty years old, but still had an eye for the ladies – and an active pen too, judging from his correspondence. Though this eye and pen are in no way to be taken as euphemistic or symbolic: Locke just wasn't that sort of person. His intentions appear to have been neither dishonourable nor even honourable – indeed one is often led to wonder whether he had any intentions at all. In one of his letters he refers to 'marriage or death (which are so very nearly the same thing)'. Then in 1682 he met Damaris Cudworth, the twenty-four-year-old daughter of a Cambridge Platonist. Damaris was by far the most intelligent woman Locke had ever met, and could converse with him on equal terms. She was 'prone to outbursts' (as was

Locke, on rare occasions), but was also possessed of emotional understanding. She appears to have fallen in love with Locke right from the start. He had retained his distinguished good looks, although his illness left him gaunt and rather frail. But Locke was only interested in his usual type of friendship – a sort of Chinese water torture by correspondence. They wrote poems to one another and exchanged letters, calling each other Philoclea and Philander (an odd choice, under the circumstances). Philoclea claimed that she was descended from Cadwallader, the legendary last king of the Ancient Britons, and Locke referred to her as his 'governess' (once again, no impropriety whatsoever should be assumed here). Then Philoclea fell out of love and decided that all she too wanted was friendship – whereupon, in the usual Restoration farce of the emotions, Locke found that he was now in love with her.

Meanwhile Shaftesbury was put on trial in

London, but was acquitted by a sympathetic jury. He at once fled for his life to Holland. (He was to die there a year later of 'gout of the stomach', a diagnosis worthy of Locke himself.) Back in England anyone associated with Shaftesbury was under suspicion. Locke too found himself in danger. At Oxford he realized that he was under surveillance by spies. According to a report from one spy: 'John Locke lives a very cunning unintelligible life.' At last a lifetime of secretiveness came into its own. The professional spies proved no match for the wily philosopher, and Locke soon gave them the slip, making his way to Holland. But only in the nick of time. The king immediately stripped Locke of his post at Christ Church, placed him on a list of eighty-four traitors, and despatched an extradition order to the Dutch government. Locke was forced to go into hiding in The Hague.

During this period Locke learned that Damaris Cudworth had married a north country widower called Sir Francis Masham. It's difficult to gauge Locke's precise feelings at this point. He loved Damaris, as he probably hadn't loved any other woman in his life. Yet he may have reasoned that he was too ill, too old and too set in his scholarly ways to make much of a husband to a woman less than half his age. But as Locke realized in his philosophy: we don't learn from reason, we learn from experience. He had never had this experience before, and my guess is that it probably hurt him deeply at the time, though he didn't show it.

In 1685 Charles II died and his Catholic brother James II ascended to the throne, confirming Shaftesbury's worst fears. Meanwhile over in Holland Locke was concentrating his energies on his philosophy. By now he was putting the finishing touches to *An Essay Concerning Human Understanding*. This opens with a delightful Epistle to the Reader, which describes the work as 'the diversion of some of my idle and heavy hours: if it has the good luck to prove so of any of thine, and thou has half so much Pleasure in reading, as I had in writing it, thou wilt as little think thy Money as I do my Pains ill bestowed'. The philosophy it contained was just as sympathetic, and as far-reaching as any since Descartes. It was not as profoundly original as Descartes' work, or as brilliant; but by dethroning reason in favour of experience it appeared to subsequent philosophers to be closer to the truth. Without Descartes there might have been no modern philosophy. But it was Locke who fathered its main line of development – the British Empiricists, who then provoked Kant to produce the greatest philosophical system of them all, which in turn gave rise to the elephantine folly of Hegel, and the consequent disbelief in all systems by anyone except Marxists and optimistic punters.

According to Locke we have no such thing

as intuitive ideas – about Right and Wrong, God etc. Despite this, Locke firmly believed in God. Descartes may have had his secret doubts on occasions; Spinoza avoided the issue by turning everything into God; and Leibnitz probably didn't believe in God, though he pretended to – but Locke was unwavering in his belief, despite the fact that there isn't really any room for God in his philosophy. 'There is nothing in the mind except what was first in the senses.' We begin with a *tabula rasa* (blank sheet). Human knowledge is derived from outer experience, and reflection (Locke's word for introspection) which enables us to discover what goes on in our minds. We use reason to draw conclusions from these experiences. In this way we arrive at generalizations, laws and the truths of mathematics.

Like Descartes, Locke believed that the empirical knowledge we gain from the senses can only be probable. But Locke didn't let this undermine all such knowledge, like Descartes. Instead of retreating into reason, he used common sense. Empirical knowledge and the knowledge we derive from it may only be probable, but by the use of intuition and deduction we can assess *how* probable. (This division between reason and common sense, which first appeared with Descartes and Locke, was to become a permanent feature of Anglo-French philosophical relations. Today it has developed to the point where the French very reasonably regard English philosophy as nothing whatsoever to do with philosophy, and English common sense confronted with French philosophy has come to an identical conclusion.)

In Book II of his *Essay Concerning Human Understanding* Locke explains that there are two distinct types of ideas which make up our empirical knowledge of the world. Simple ideas, such as colour, heat and cold, and taste are indivisible. Complex ideas, on the other hand, are made up of combinations of these ideas. Such combinations may result in things which have no corresponding entity in the real world – such as ghosts or UFOs.

Locke also distinguishes between the primary and secondary qualities of objects. (Here he drew heavily on the notions of Galileo and the Gassendists.) Primary qualities are those which are possessed by all objects, regardless of what they are. These include such qualities as extension, solidity and mobility. The ideas produced in us by our perception of these qualities closely resemble the qualities themselves. In secondary qualities, such as taste, colour and smell, this is not the case. The taste and smell of a bad egg are merely powers in this objectionable object which produce ideas that do not resemble their cause.

Locke's thinking on these matter reflects the revolution which was taking place in the science of the period. It is no accident that

Locke was a contemporary of great scientific thinkers ranging from Galileo to Newton.

In 1688 the so-called Glorious Revolution took place. The English decided that they'd had enough of James II. The Dutch Protestant William, Prince of Orange was asked to take over, but only on certain strict conditions which left the effective power in the hands of Parliament. William sailed from Holland, and a few months later his wife Mary followed. Locke accompanied Mary, Princess of Orange and returned to England in the wake of the Glorious Revolution (so-called because it took place without bloodshed).

Locke was now free to publish *An Essay Concerning Human Understanding*, which he did in 1689 (despite the date 1690 which appears on the frontispiece). In direct contravention of Locke's wish to clear away 'some of the rubbish that lies in the way of knowledge', his work soon began attracting the usual barrage of criticism, most notably from

Leibnitz and Berkeley. In the hope of fore-
stalling any more rubbish, Locke quickly
began making heavy alterations in his copy
of the book, rebutting each of these criticisms
as they appeared – before any further edition
was published. (This *ad hoc* philosophy can
be observed in the British Museum's first edition, which has long emendations in Locke's
own hand.)

Sixteen eighty-nine also saw the publication of Locke's other great work, his *Two
Treatises of Government*. Locke had initially
written this in 1681, but the times had been
far too dangerous for the publication of such
a liberal political work. He had rewritten
parts of this manuscript during his enforced
stay in Holland; and made further alterations,
taking into account his approval of the Glorious Revolution, when he returned to England.
This caused several critics to accuse him of
writing this work simply to justify the Glorious Revolution. This was not the case. In this

work he justifies revolution, but he had not written it to justify the Glorious Revolution – more to prepare the way for it.

Others accused Locke of writing this work in the hope of receiving a post from the new king. Nothing could have been further from the truth. Locke in fact even turned down a job from William. When he was offered the post of British ambassador to the court of Frederick III of Brandenburg, he politely declined. An ambassador needed to socialize, and Locke declared that he wasn't up to the 'warm drinking' habits of the Germans. William would be better off sending an ambassador who was willing to 'drink his share' instead of 'the soberest man in England'.

The first of Locke's *Two Treatises of Government* is a refutation of the ideas of Robert Filmer, a highly popular political theorist of the period – whose fame died long before his audience. (Locke's secretive practices had ensured that he was spared such fickleness.) Filmer was a neo-Hobbesian who believed in the Divine Right of Kings. Locke had long since suppressed his Hobbesian ideas (along with *almost* all manuscript evidence of them), and this was his attempt to prevent a viable alternative.

In the second treatise Locke attempts to discover the roots of government. In the original state of nature people were free and equal. But such freedom and equality were largely theoretical. People were simply unable to get along together without infringing each other's rights. Locke believed that the law of nature grants us each natural rights. We have a right to life and a right to liberty, as long as this doesn't infringe on the liberty and natural rights of others. But without an element of coercion we are unable to enjoy these natural rights. To do so, we must join together in a social contract. This guarantees our natural rights by establishing a government which enforces laws protecting them. A framework of security is established. Under this condition our theoretical liberty may be restricted, but our actual liberty is increased.

The consent of the people is the sole basis for this government's authority. Locke makes this perfectly clear: 'whosoever in authority exceeds the power given him by the law, and makes use of the force he has under his command to compass that upon the subject which the law allows not . . . may be opposed as any other man, who by force invades the right of another'. If the government, or ruler, violates the rights of individual citizens, then the people have the right to revolt and get rid of this ruler or government. 'To take away and destroy the property of the people, or to reduce them to slavery [puts a ruler] into a state of war with the people, who are thereupon absolved from any further obedience, and are left to the common refuge, which God hath provided for all men against force and violence.' In other words, revolution.

Locke believed that government should act solely for the purpose for which it was originally formed – namely, the protection of life, liberty and property. 'When any number of men have so consented to make one community or government, they are thereby presently incorporated and make one body politic, wherein the majority have a right to act and conclude the rest.' This laid the foundation upon which modern liberal democracy was built. These were the ideas which a century later inspired the American Declaration of Independence and the French Revolution. Such sentiments may sound simplistic in the modern era of populous technological democracies – but they remain very much the beliefs and principles of the citizens who inhabit them.

Although Locke's girlfriend had now married and become Lady Masham, he still kept in contact with her. There was obviously a deep rapport between the philosopher and his accommodating intellectual lady friend.

However, she never completely converted to Locke's Empiricism, faithfully retaining an element of her father's Platonism – a combination which would have taxed any but the most accommodating of intellects.

Lady Masham appeared to understand Locke and his emotional needs like no other, and he obviously blossomed in her company. Locke became a regular visitor to Sir Francis and Lady Masham's country house Oates, which was twenty miles north-east of London in Essex. The country air suited him, and after a couple of years the Mashams invited him to make Oates his home.

This is a story with a happy ending. Locke gratefully accepted the Mashams' invitation, moved in, and they all appeared to enjoy their *ménage à trois*. Sir Francis was the local member of Parliament for the county of Essex. He was a typical English gentleman: charming, thick as a brick, and a convinced philistine. He was only too pleased that his intellectual wife had someone to talk to, leaving him free to go up to London on parliamentary business. He seems to have embodied all the best qualities of tolerance, such as Locke's philosophy proposed, in his dealings with its author. They had nothing to say to each other, and indeed seemingly talked very little to one another, as they went about their separate lives. Whether this was due to mutual respect, or indifference, is difficult to tell. This was a quintessentially English *ménage à trois*, and there was no hint of scandal.

Oates was a modest country house dating from Tudor times. It was built of local red brick, had Gothic battlements, and was encompassed by a moat. It was situated at High Lever, a village deep in the Essex countryside between Harlow and Chipping Ongar. The house had a pleasant rose garden with a lawn beside a pond, where Locke liked to sit and read in the summer. (For some unaccountable reason the whole place was flattened in 1802 and the site was left derelict. The lawns reverted to water meadows, the pond became clogged with weeds, and much of the moat silted up. The site of the house is now a grassy meadow in open countryside, beside a small lake which is home to a sizeable colony of ducks and geese. Whilst I was walking across this meadow recently on a cold grey February morning I came across a small patch of rubble breaking the surface amongst the grass. This contained several fragments of old red brick: all that apparently remained of Oates.)

Locke moved into two rooms on the first floor off the panelled entrance hall, bringing with him a few pieces of his own furniture and the usual bare essentials required by any philosopher (5,000 books, according to his biographer). He paid one pound a week for his keep and that of his servant, and one shilling a week for the stabling of his horse.

But Locke had not retired. Far from it. He

was now looked upon as the intellectual *éminence grise* of the Whigs, the main party in Parliament, and was constantly being consulted on policy matters. He appears to have travelled to London frequently, but always returned to the country when his asthma attacks became too much. He even took on a senior post at the Board of Trade and Plantations.

In the middle of winter 1698 Locke was summoned for an urgent meeting with the king at Kensington Palace. Reluctantly he clambered into the coach, his chest was heavily wrapped in layers of rugs, and he set off on the long drive down the ice-rutted turnpike across the bleak snow-covered countryside. For some reason Locke always kept the purpose of this visit to the king a secret, which he wouldn't even confide to Lady Masham. However, most sources agree that he was probably offered, and politely turned down, the job of ambassador to France, a post which was more than ornamental in those days.

In between his public duties Locke mixed with the intellectuals of his day. This species, now extinct in Britain, flourished in seventeenth-century London – without any question of there being two cultures. Locke would have met most of the leading literary and scientific figures of his time: not including, one hopes, the dreadful Dryden, who was by now reduced to the ignominious task of translating Virgil, a fate he thoroughly deserved. Locke became particularly friendly with Newton, who often came to visit him at Oates. Those who wonder what the two greatest minds of their time discussed, while sitting in the garden watching gravity at work in the orchard, will be disappointed. Newton tried to explain gravity to Locke, but the philosopher had to pretend to understand – the only example of intellectual deceit by Locke which I have so far come across. Instead the Laurel and Hardy of contemporary learning (now look what a fine mess they've got us into) spent their time discussing the Epistles of St Paul. These were a great favourite with Newton, who devoted much of his energy to writing commentaries on the Bible. He remained convinced to his dying day that this was his real life's work, for which he would be remembered in the years to come, long after gravity had been forgotten.

In 1699 Locke was finally forced to resign from his post at the Board of Trade and Plantations. He was now sixty-seven and his asthma was gradually worsening. He was to live for another four years at Oates, industriously writing on such diverse matters as religious tolerance, the size of the groat, and the effect of interest rates on the likes of Sir Francis. Finally, on 28 October 1704, he died – having spent the previous night with his frail wheezing frame supported in the arms of Lady Masham.

Locke was buried at High Lever church,

where you can still see his redbrick tomb today, behind some railings against the flintstone south wall. After he died Lady Masham abandoned her husband at Oates and went to live in Bath – giving rise to speculation that her attachment to Locke may have been more than Platonic. Either way, all three of them are now buried at High Lever church, Lady Masham lying dutifully beside her husband in the nave.

Afterword

Locke's life spanned the era from Galileo to Newton. It is no coincidence that during his lifetime heliocentricity became accepted, calculus and celestial gravity were discovered, and the circulation of the blood was detected. Such things were literally unthinkable in terms of Aristotle and Scholasticism (which for instance believed that everything was made up of earth, air, fire and water). The emerging modern world was completely different from one which was lived in by the medievalists. This new world needed a new way of thinking, and in philosophy this was provided by Locke. His *Essay Concerning Human Understanding* was to be the most influential philosophical work throughout Europe for the next hundred years.

It is also no coincidence that Locke witnessed the last civil war in England and the first successful revolution in modern Europe. As we have seen, Locke's political thought laid the foundations for the American Declaration of Independence, the French Revolution and liberal democracy. But these two elements in Locke's thinking – the political and the purely philosophical – were not disparate. Luther had liberated people from the authority of the Church, allowing them private judgement and a personal conscience. In the same way, Locke delivered them from 'the thralldom of error and prejudice'. What was happening in Europe was nothing less than the emergence of the individual. This new evolutionary freak – widespread individuality – sought to express itself. Locke's philosophy showed it the way. On the one hand liberty of thought, on the other liberty of action. The two went hand in hand: in life, as well as in the works of Locke. This was his gift to the world. And no matter how succeeding generations of critics may have picked holes in his philosophy or rendered it outmoded, this gift will remain for ever undeniable.

Key Quotations

He who has raised himself above the alms-basket, and, not content to live lazily on scraps of begged opinions, sets his own thoughts on work, to find and follow truth, will (whatever he lights on) not miss the hunter's satisfaction; every moment of his pursuit will reward his pains with some delight; and he will have reason to think his time not ill spent, even when he cannot much boast of any great acquisition.

from *An Essay Concerning Human Understanding*, Epistle to the Reader

There are [no innate principles] to which all mankind give an universal consent. I shall begin with the speculative, and instance in those magnified principles of demonstration, *Whatsoever is, is* and *It is impossible for the same thing to be and not to be*, which of all others I think have the most allowed title to innate. These have so settled a reputation of maxims universally received that it will, no doubt, be thought strange if anyone should seem to question it. But yet I take the liberty to say that these propositions are so far from having an universal assent, that there are a great part of mankind to whom they are not so much as known.

For, first, it is evident that all *children* and *idiots* have not the least apprehension or thought of them.

Ibid., Book 1, ch. 2 , secs 4, 5

Let us then suppose that the mind be, as we say, white paper void of all characters, without any *ideas*. How comes it to be furnished? Whence comes it by that vast store which the busy and boundless fancy of man has painted on it with an almost endless variety? Whence has it all the materials of reason and knowledge? To this I answer, in one word, from *experience*; in that all our knowledge is founded, and from that it ultimately derives itself.

Ibid., Bk 2, ch. 1, sec 2

Our observation, employed either about *external sensible objects, or about the internal operations of our minds perceived and reflected on by ourselves, is that which supplies our understanding with all the materials of thinking.* These two are the fountains of knowledge, from whence all the *ideas* we have, or can naturally have, do spring.

Ibid., Bk 2, ch. 1, sec 2

The power to produce any *idea* in our mind, I call *quality* of the subject wherein that power is. Thus a snowball having the power to produce in us the *ideas of white, cold* and *round*, the powers to produce those ideas in us, as they are in the snowball, I call *qualities*; and as they are sensations, or perceptions, in our understanding, I call them *ideas*.

Ibid., Bk 2, ch. 8, sec 8

Such *qualities* which in truth are nothing in the objects themselves but powers to produce various sensations in us by their *primary qualities*, i.e. by the bulk, figure, texture, and motion of their insensible parts, as colours, sounds, tastes, etc. These I call *secondary qualities* . . . For the power in fire to produce a new colour, or consistency in wax or clay, by its primary qualities, is as much a quality in fire as the power it has to produce in me a new *idea* or sensation of warmth or burning, which I felt not before, by the same primary qualities, viz. the bulk, texture and motion of its insensible parts.

Ibid., Bk 2, ch. 8, sec 10

The ideas of *primary qualities* of bodies, *are resemblances* of them, and their patterns do really exist in the bodies themselves; but the *ideas* produced in us by these *secondary qualities have no resemblance* of them at all. There is nothing like our *ideas*, existing in the bodies themselves.

Ibid., Bk 2, ch. 8, sec 15

As simple ideas are observed to exist in various combinations united together; so the mind has a power to consider several of them united together, as one *idea*; and that not only are they united in external objects, but as itself has joined them. *Ideas* thus made up of several simple ones put together, I call *complex*, such as are *beauty, gratitude, a man, an army, the universe*; which, though complicated of various simple *ideas*, or *complex ideas* made up of simple ones, yet are, when the mind pleases, considered each by itself as one entire thing, and signified by one name.

Ibid., Bk 2, ch. 12, sec 1

We can have no *idea* of the place of the universe, though we can of all the parts in it; because beyond that, we have not the *idea* of any fixed, distinct, particular beings, in reference to which, we can imagine it to have any relation of distance, but all beyond it is one uniform space or expansion, wherein the mind finds no variety, no marks.

Ibid., Bk 2, ch. 13, sec 10

Some of our *ideas* have a natural correspondence and connexion one with another; it is the office and excellence of our reason to trace these, and hold them together in that union and correspondence which is founded in their peculiar beings. Besides this, there is another connexion of *ideas* wholly owing to chance or custom; *ideas* that in themselves are not at all of kin, come to be so united in some men's minds that it is very hard to separate them, they always keep in company, and the one no sooner at any time comes into the understanding but its associate appears with it ... That there are such associations of them made by custom in the minds of most men, I think nobody will question who has well considered himself or others; and to this, perhaps, might be justly attributed most of the sympathies and antipathies observable in men, which work as strongly and produce as regular effects as if they were natural; and are therefore called so, though they at first had no other original but the accidental connexion of two *ideas*.

Ibid., Bk 2, ch. 33, sec 5–7

Political power then I take to be *a right* of making laws with penalties of death, and consequently all less penalties, for the regulating and preserving of property, and of employing the force of the community, in the execution of such laws, and in the defence of the commonwealth from foreign injury, and all this only for the public good.

Two Treatises of Government,
2nd ch. 1, sec 3

To understand political power right, and derive it from its original, we must consider what state all men are naturally in, and that is, a *state of perfect freedom* to order their actions, and dispose of their possessions, and person as they think fit, within the bounds of the law of nature, without asking leave, or depending upon the will of any other man.

A *state* also of *equality*, wherein all the power and jurisdiction is reciprocal, no one having more than another . . .

Ibid., 2nd ch 2, sec 1 1–8

The *state of nature* has a law of nature to govern it, which obliges everyone: and reason, which is that law, teaches all mankind, who will but consult it, that being all equal and independent, no one ought to harm another in his life, health, liberty, or possessions.

Ibid., 2nd ch. 2, sec 6 1 6–10

Civil government is the proper remedy for the inconveniences of the state of nature, which must certainly be great, where men may be judges in their own case, since 'tis easily to be imagined, that he who was so unjust as to do his brother an injury, will scarce be so just as to condemn himself for it.

Ibid., 2nd ch. 2, sec 13 1 10–14

'Tis often asked as a mighty objection, *Where are*, or ever were, there any *men in such a state of nature*? To which it may suffice as an answer at present; that since all *princes* and rulers of *independent* governments all through the world, are in a state of nature, 'tis plain the world never was, nor ever will be, without numbers of men in that state.

Ibid., 2nd ch. 2, sec 14 1 1–6

The *natural liberty* of man is to be free from any superior power on earth, and not to be under the will or legislative authority of man, but to have only the law of nature for his rule. The liberty of man, in society, is to be under no other legislative power but that established, by consent, in the commonwealth, nor under the dominion of any will, or restraint of any law, but what the legislative will enact, according to the trust put in it.

Ibid., 2nd ch. 4, sec 1 1–8

Chronology of significant philosophical dates

6th century BC	The start of Western philosophy with Thales of Miletus.
end of 6th century BC	Death of Pythagoras.
399 BC	Socrates sentenced to death in Athens.
c.387 BC	Plato founds the Academy in Athens, the first university.
335 BC	Aristotle founds the Lyceum in Athens, rival school to the Academy.
324 AD	Emperor Constantine moves capital of Roman Empire to Byzantium.
400 AD	St Augustine writes his

Confessions.
Philosophy absorbed into
Christian theology.

410 AD Sack of Rome by Visigoths
heralds start of Dark Ages.

529 AD Closure of Academy in Athens
by Emperor Justinian marks
end of Hellenic thought.

mid 13th Thomas Aquinas writes his
century commentaries on Aristotle. Era
of Scholasticism.

1453 Fall of Byzantium to Turks,
end of Byzantine Empire.

1492 Columbus reaches America.
Renaissance in Florence and
revival of interest in Greek
learning.

1543 Copernicus publishes *De
revolutionibus orbium
caelestium* (On the Revolution
of the Celestial Orbs) proving

	mathematically that the earth revolves around the sun.
1633	Galileo forced by Church to recant heliocentric theory of the Universe.
1641	Descartes publishes his *Meditations*, the start of modern philosophy.
1677	Death of Spinoza allows publication of his *Ethics*.
1687	Newton publishes *Principia*, introducing concept of gravity.
1689	Locke publishes *Essay Concerning Human Understanding*. Start of Empiricism.
1710	Berkeley publishes *Principles of Human Knowledge*, advancing Empiricism to new extremes.
1716	Death of Leibnitz.

1739–40   Hume publishes *Treatise of Human Nature*, taking Empiricism to its logical limits.

1781   Kant, woken from his 'dogmatic slumbers' by Hume, publishes *Critique of Pure Reason*. Great era of German metaphysics begins.

1807   Hegel publishes *The Phenomenology of Mind*: high point of German metaphysics.

1818   Schopenhauer publishes *The World as Will and Representation*, introducing Indian philosophy into German metaphysics.

1889   Nietzsche, having declared 'God is dead', succumbs to madness in Turin.

1921   Wittgenstein publishes *Tractatus Logico-*

Philosophicus, claiming the 'final solution' to the problems of philosophy.

1920s   Vienna Circle propound Logical Positivism.

1927   Heidegger publishes *Sein und Zeit* (Being and Time), heralding split between analytical and continental philosophy.

1943   Sartre publishes *L'Être et le néant* (Being and Nothingness), advancing Heidegger's thought and instigating Existentialism.

1953   Posthumous publication of Wittgenstein's *Philosophical Investigations*. High era of Linguistic Analysis.